CLOSE HARMONY
Ladies Barbershop Songbook

Arranged by
Nicholas Hare

for SSAA
close-harmony group
or women's choir

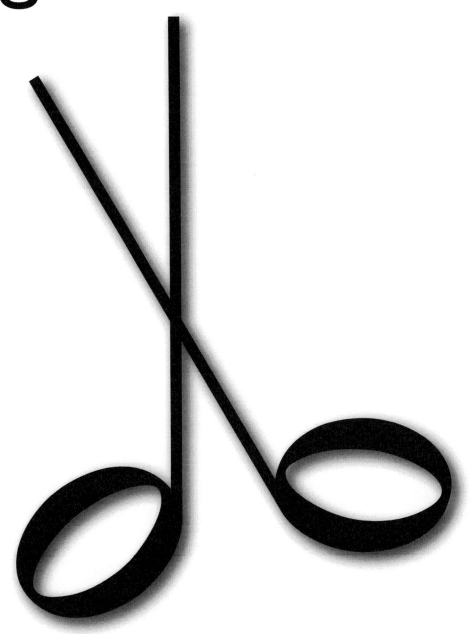

Novello Publishing Limited

Order No. NOV200199

Preface

'Close Harmony' offers unaccompanied arrangements
of a variety of well-loved songs, from the 1920s to the 1970s.
Performances should work equally well with choirs or just
four voices.

The arranger has endeavoured to share the interest amongst
all the voice parts, but each singer should be aware at all times
of who has the melody, so that it is allowed to stand out.

Blend and balance of the harmony is another important element
in successful performance of this music, and vibrato should be kept
in check, so that the chords are clean and perfectly in tune.

The various 'vocalisations' (ah, ooh, mm, etc.) may be
considered as suggestions only, and varied according to the
performance conditions.

Cover design by Michael Bell Design.
Music setting by New Notations.

ISBN 978-0-85360-787-8

This book © Copyright 1997 Novello & Company
Limited. Published in Great Britain by Novello
Publishing Limited.

Exclusive distributors:
Hal Leonard
7777 West Bluemound Road, Milwaukee, WI 53213
Email: info@halleonard.com

Hal Leonard Europe Limited
42 Wigmore Street Maryleborne, London, WIU 2 RY
Email: info@halleonardeurope.com

Hal Leonard Australia Pty. Ltd.
4 Lentara Court Cheltenham, Victoria, 9132 Australia
Email: info@halleonard.com.au

Can't Help Lovin' Dat Man
page 4
Adopt a slightly free approach for the first time through, with a very smooth creamy blend. On the repeat, sung with a bit of swing, the rhythms can perhaps be a little more pointed. Tune the chromatic harmonies carefully, occasionally bringing out a spicy clash (eg. 3rd beat in bar 4). In bars 17-22 the moving parts (eg. Soprano 2, bars 17 and 18) should stand out a little.

Summertime
page 6
The feel to this can be very similar to the previous number. Make very small breaks (not necessarily breaths) between the accompanying ooh's and don't over-emphasize the hairpins. Sing very legato when all voices have the same text at bar 33.

Fly Me To The Moon (In Other Words)
page 9
A particular feature of this one is the smooth flowing lines. Each voice part should ebb and flow individually until they come together for the final phrase.

Big Spender
page 11
This should be quite raunchy! The melody, carried mostly by Alto 2, could have a touch of huskiness. Make the most of the 'blue' notes (here notated as B naturals). At bar 24 the mood can become somewhat skittish, and towards the end things become a little 'catty' as each voice presses her case in turn (who's going to get that cream !)!

The Sound Of Silence
page 14
Make the accompaniment very smooth in· verse 1. It should become more rhythmic at verse 2 where Alto 2 has an important bass role - come in positively on the first beat at bar 18 to change the mood. Make sure that the evocative words are clearly heard.

Diamonds Are A Girl's Best Friend
page 19
Some of this has quite a military mood, so the opening phrase can be sung with some emphasis. However, this mood needs to change according to the words, eg. at bars 9 and 36.

Tonight
page 22
The accompanying parts should be very rhythmic in order to drive forward the melody (which is divided amongst all four voices). Perhaps rehearse in 4/4 to get the syncopations accurate. At bar 56 notice the emphasis of 'address' falls on the first syllable. Hold the last chord firmly to the end.

He Was Beautiful (Cavatina)
page 27
Here is another smooth, flowing number, oozing in nostalgia. It is marked Lento, but don't overdo it! Inject a little more urgency at bar 43.

I'm Gonna Wash That Man Right Outa My Hair
page 31
A lively 2-in-a-bar show tune. The dotted rhythms are swung, but equal quavers (eighth-notes) (eg. bars 12-13 and 15-16) should be sung equal as written. Alto 2 has an important role in keeping the rhythm absolutely steady. The changes of time signature at bars 33 and 94 are easy to manage if you remember to keep a constant 2-in-a-bar. The Allegro at bar 48 is a completely new tempo and bars 64-71 can be very free, returning to the tempo of the opening at bar 72. At the end keep the tempo and tone going right to the final cut-off.

Do You Want To Know A Secret?
page 38
The introduction can be sung very freely, in natural speech rhythm if you like. From bar 5 the pulse should be steady, as set by Alto 1. The melody is entirely in Soprano 1, so balance should not present a particular problem.

We'll Meet Again
page 41
The melody starts off in Soprano 2 and moves to Alto 1 at bar 9. Work for a good blend of tone, with careful tuning of chromatic harmony (enjoy the juicy clashes, eg. at bars 7 and 10!). Bars 24-30 can be gently swung.

Sailing
page 44
Throughout this piece there is contrast between smooth, flowing lines for some voices while others (especially Alto 2 from bar 21) have more rhythmic figures. Alto 2 goes quite low in places: ideally this should be sung as written, but if there is a problem with projecting the sound at this low pitch some alternatives are given.

CAN'T HELP LOVIN' DAT MAN

from *Show Boat*

Words by Oscar Hammerstein II
Music by Jerome Kern
arr. Nicholas Hare

Moderato (1st time **rubato,** 2nd time **with a gentle swing**)

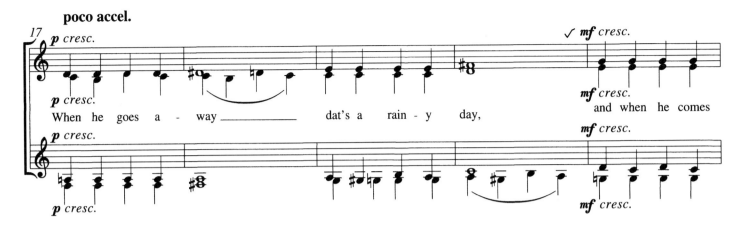

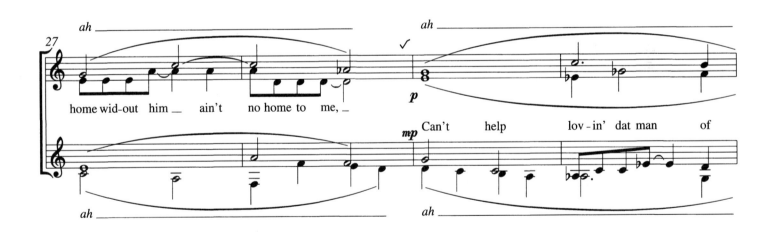

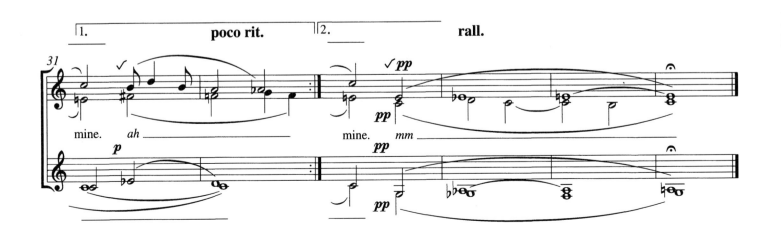

SUMMERTIME

from *Porgy and Bess*

Words by Ira Gershwin,
DuBose & Dorothy Hayward
Music by George Gershwin
arr. Nicholas Hare

FLY ME TO THE MOON
(In Other Words)

Words & Music by Bart Howard
arr. Nicholas Hare

BIG SPENDER

from *Sweet Charity*

Words by Dorothy Fields
Music by Cy Coleman
arr. Nicholas Hare

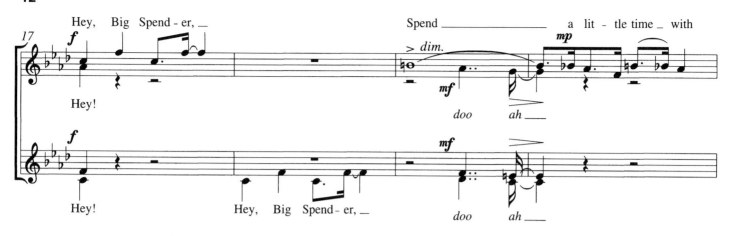

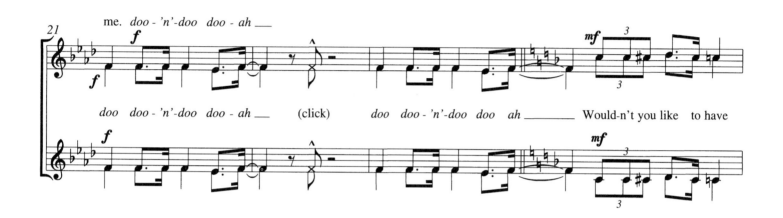

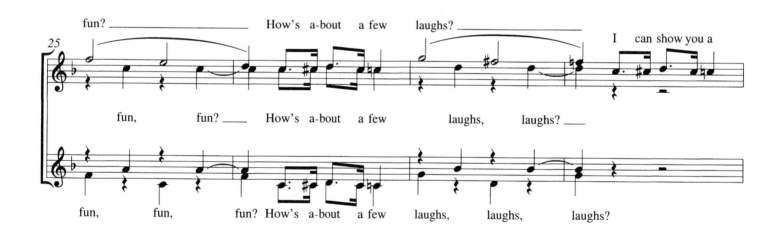

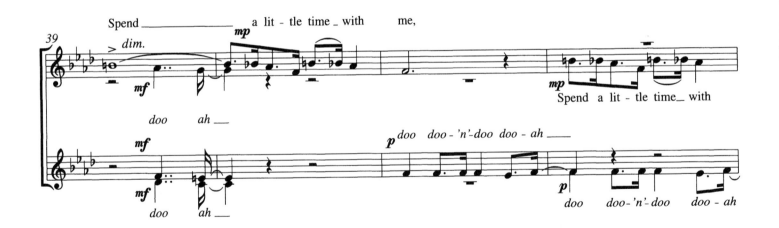

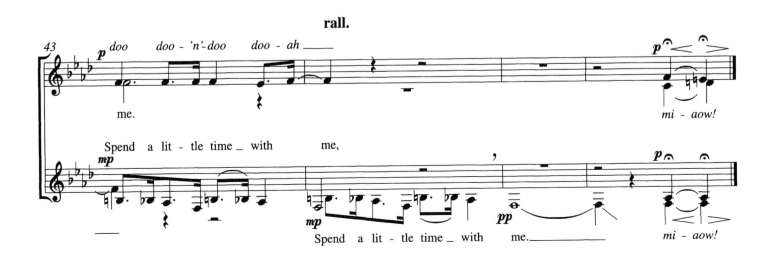

THE SOUND OF SILENCE

Words and Music by Paul Simon
arr. Nicholas Hare

Moderato espressivo

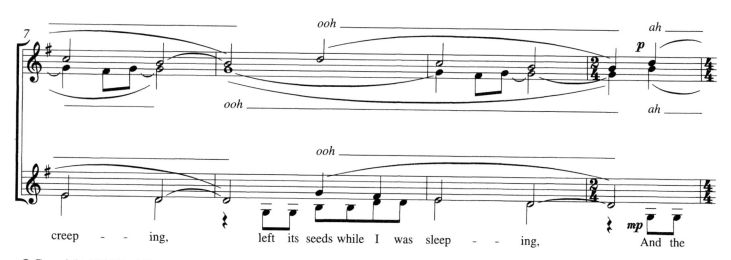

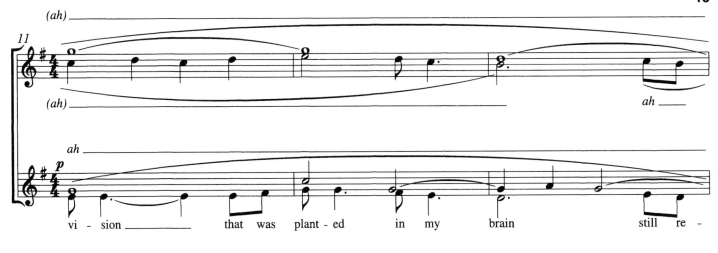

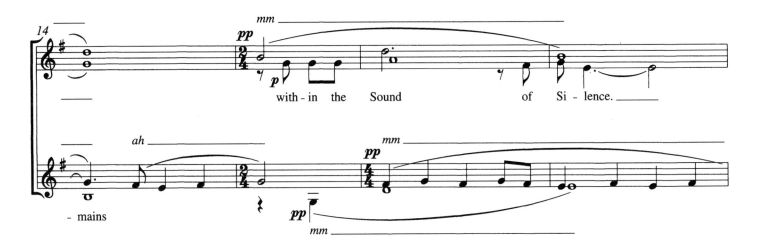

more rhythmic

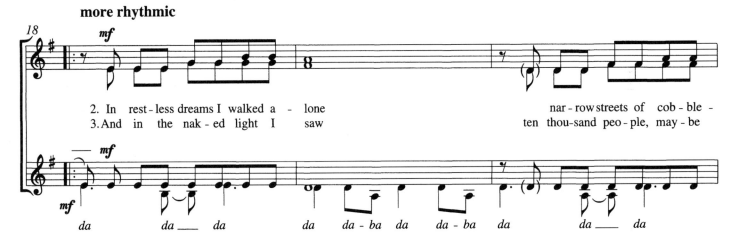

Hear my words that I might teach you, — Take my arms that I might

hear my words that I might teach you, — Oh — take my arms that I might

reach you." — But my words like si - lent rain-drops

reach you." — ooh — But my words like si - lent rain-drops

fell, ooh and ech-oed in the wells of

ooh ech-oed — ooh

fell, ooh ooh ech - oed ooh

si - lence. —

5. And the peo-ple bowed and prayed to the ne - on god they

da da — da da da - ba da da - ba da da — da

DIAMONDS ARE A GIRL'S BEST FRIEND

from *Gentlemen Prefer Blondes*

Words by Leo Robin
Music by Jule Styne
arr. Nicholas Hare

16

dim. *p*

jew - els; _____ A kiss on the hand may be
flick - er; _____ There may come a time when a

dim. *p*

ah _____ A kiss
There may

22 *mf* *dim.*

quite Con - ti - nen - tal, But dia - monds are a girl's best friend, _____
lass needs a law - yer, But dia - monds are a girl's best friend, _____

mf *dim.*

But
But

27 *p*

— A kiss may be grand But it won't pay the rent - al on your
— There may come a time When a hard - boiled em - ploy - er thinks you're

p

A kiss
There may

32 *cresc.*

hum - ble flat _____ Or help you at the Au - to - mat.
aw - ful nice, _____ But get that "ice" or else no dice.

cresc.

flat _____
nice, _____

TONIGHT
from *West Side Story*

Words by Stephen Sondheim
Music by Leonard Bernstein
arr. Nicholas Hare

Lento

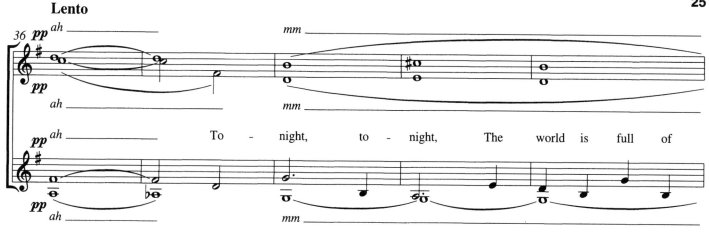

Tonight, to-night, The world is full of

accel. poco a poco

light, ah ba ba ba ba ba ba ba ba ba ba ba ba ba ah
With suns and moons all o - ver the place.

a tempo (allegro)

To - night, to - night, The world is wild and
ba ba ba ba ba ba ba ba ba ba ba ba ba ba ba ba ba ba ba ba ba

bright, Go - ing mad, shoot - ing sparks in - to space.

HE WAS BEAUTIFUL
(Cavatina)

Words by Cleo Laine
Music by Stanley Myers
arr. Nicholas Hare

I'M GONNA WASH THAT MAN RIGHT OUT-A MY HAIR

from *South Pacific*

Words by Oscar Hammerstein II
Music by Richard Rodgers
arr. Nicholas Hare

DO YOU WANT TO KNOW A SECRET

Words and Music by John Lennon
and Paul McCartney
arr. Nicholas Hare

You'll ne-ver know how much I real - ly love you, You'll ne-ver know how much I

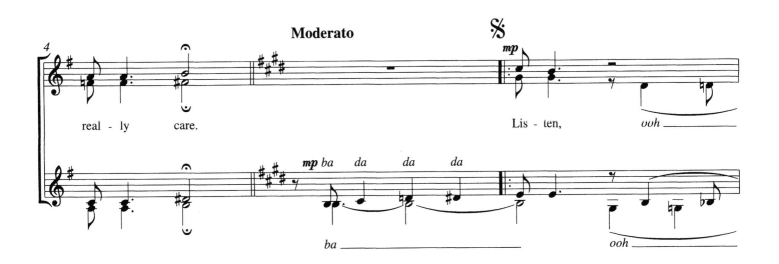

real - ly care. Lis - ten, ooh

ba da da da
ba ooh

do you want to know a se - cret? ooh Do you pro - mise not to

ooh

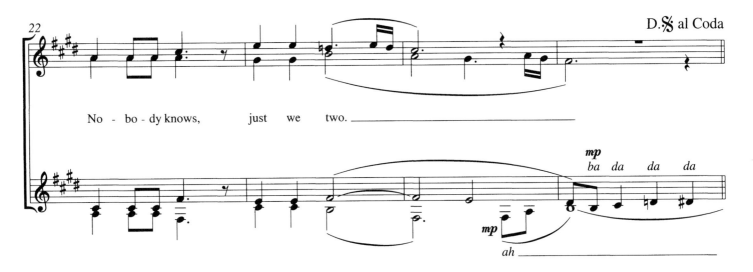

D.S. al Coda

No - bo - dy knows, just we two. _____

ba da da da

ah _____

CODA

you. _____ *ooh* _____ *ooh* _____

you *doo doo doo doo* *ooh* *doo doo doo doo doo*

you. *doo doo doo doo* *ah* _____ *doo doo doo doo doo*

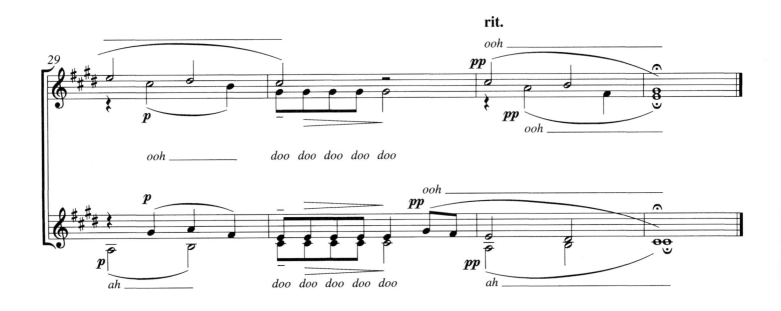

rit.

ooh _____

ooh _____

ooh _____ *doo doo doo doo doo* *ooh* _____

ah _____ *doo doo doo doo doo* *ah* _____

WE'LL MEET AGAIN

**Words and Music by Ross Parker
and Hughie Charles**
arr. Nicholas Hare

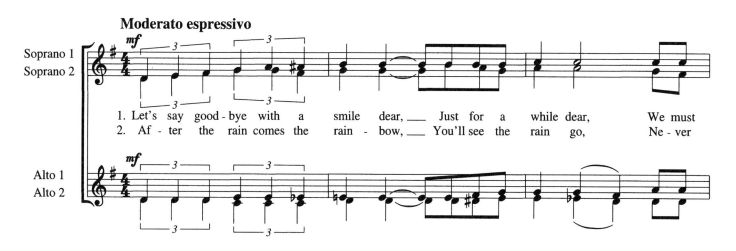

1. Let's say good-bye with a smile dear, ___ Just for a while dear, We must
2. Af-ter the rain comes the rain-bow, ___ You'll see the rain go, Ne-ver

part, oh ___ Don't let the part-ing up-set you, ___ I'll not for-
fear, oh ___ We two can wait for to-mor-row, ___ Good-bye to

-get you, sweet-heart. _____ We'll meet a-gain, don't know
sor-row my dear. _____

27

I won't be long, __ I won't be long. They'll be hap - py to know __ that as

won't be long.

30

cresc. *f*

you saw me go, __ I was sing - ing this song. _____ We'll meet a -

cresc. *più f*

34

a -

- gain, don't know where, don't know when, _____ But I know we'll meet a -

38

1. 2.

- gain some day. *ah* _____ - gain some day. _____

- gain __ some day. *ah* _____ - gain some day, some __ day.

- gain some sun - ny day. _____ - gain some sun - ny day, some __ day.

day. *ah* _____

SAILING

Words and Music by Gavin Sutherland
arr. Nicholas Hare

Slow and expressive, but rhythmic

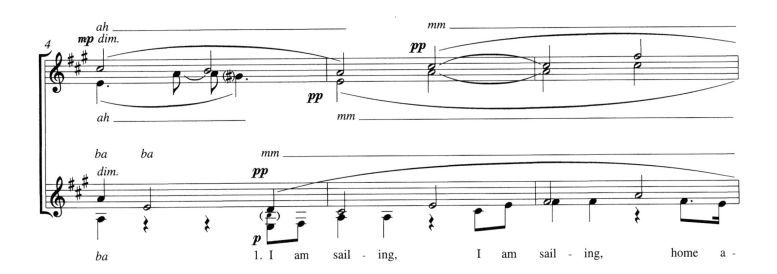

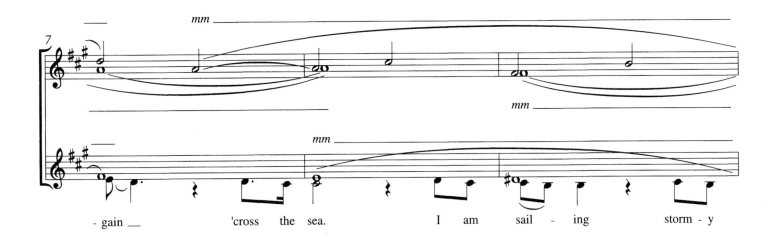

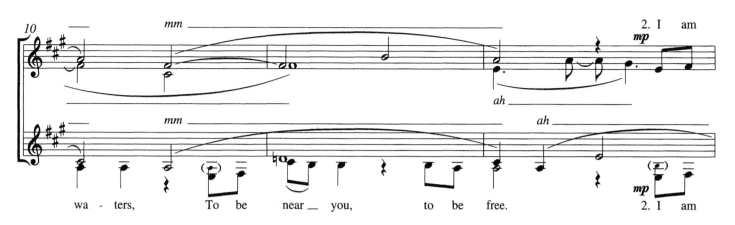

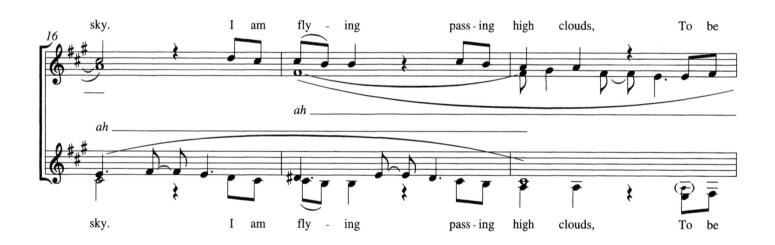

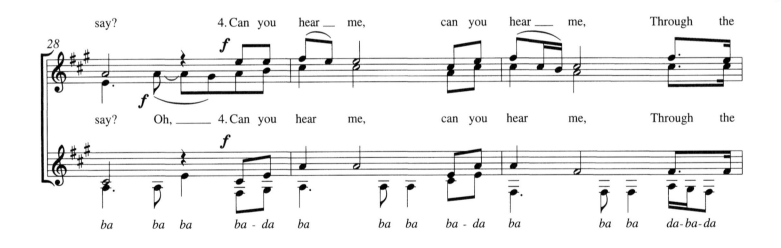

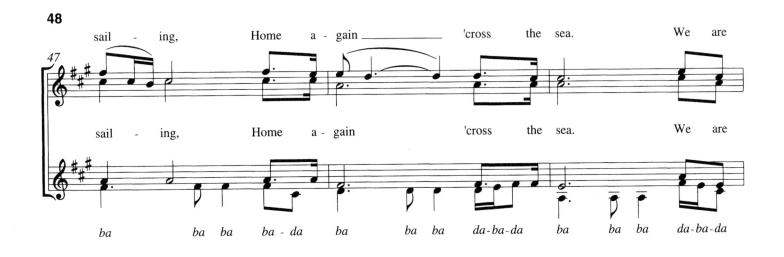